ROCK & ROLL
HALL OF FAMERS

Bruce Springsteen

SUSIE DERKINS

the rosen publishing group's
rosen
central

*To Mom, Dad, Susan, Jakey, Rachel, Kerry, and especially John,
and to all of the other wonderful people I know and love in and
from New Jersey*

Published in 2002 by The Rosen Publishing Group, Inc.
29 East 21st Street, New York, NY 10010

First Edition

Library of Congress Cataloging-in-Publication Data

Derkins, Susie.
Bruce Springsteen / by Susie Derkins. — 1st ed.
p. cm. — (Rock & roll hall of famers)
Includes discography (p. 104), bibliographical references
(p. 109), and index.
ISBN 0-8239-3522-1 (alk. paper)
1. Springsteen, Bruce—Juvenile literature. 2. Rock
musicians—United States—Biography—Juvenile
literature. I. Title. II. Series.
ML3930.S72 D47 2001
782.42166'092—dc21

2001004609

Manufactured in the United States of America

CONTENTS

For nearly three decades, Bruce Springsteen has been a singer-songwriter, rock star, and working-class hero.

Introduction

Rock and roll legend Bruce Springsteen—the Boss—is loved and respected by millions of music fans around the world for his sensitive, passionate songs, as well as his onstage enthusiasm. Within his generation, Bruce is as famous a rock and roll icon as Elvis Presley. He is honored by fans and critics alike for the Bob Dylan–like purity and creativity of his work, especially his sensitive, poetic lyrics.

Bruce Springsteen

Perhaps best known for fist-pumping rock anthems like "Born to Run"—the "number one pop song of all time," according to a 1995 BBC Radio One poll—Bruce Springsteen is also the quiet, thoughtful author of heartfelt songs that reflect his life and past. He writes songs that support small-town life and old-fashioned values like loyalty, community, and caring for one's fellow men and women.

Bruce's career, steadily building since the early 1970s, has been a revolving door of touring and recording. By any definition, he is a workaholic. His recording output has been nothing short of phenomenal, with hundreds of songs created over the past thirty years. And his live shows are simply legendary. Performances are typically three-hour spectacles full of athletic jumps, kicks, and hollers. Bruce has also maintained a steady commitment to social causes, which he supports through benefit shows, records, and donations to his favorite charities.

As Bruce has grown older, he has hardly mellowed. He is still famous for his energetic live shows and his boyish good looks. But he has

While Bruce Springsteen has come a long way in his career, he has remained down-to-earth and close to his roots.

matured a bit, taking the time to have a family with wife (and E Street Band backup singer) Patti Scialfa. Today, Bruce has homes in Rumson and Colts Neck, New Jersey, two towns very close to where he grew up. He still hangs out with most of the same friends as when he was first getting started in his career, and he still loves showing up unannounced at

Asbury Park rock clubs to play surprise gigs with fellow local musicians.

Bruce Springsteen is a rock and roll legend and an exceptional artist—perhaps ironically, because he has remained so down-to-earth. Regular people all over the world appreciate and respect the "common person" values that Bruce embodies in his work. There simply is no other rock idol like the Boss.

Growin' Up

Bruce Springsteen was born on September 23, 1949, in Long Branch, New Jersey, to Douglas and Adele Springsteen. He was raised in nearby Freehold, New Jersey, a small town in the east-central part of the state, with his two younger sisters, Pamela and Virginia. When Bruce was growing up, Freehold was an industrial town of about 25,000 people. Most of them were poor or working class, holding jobs in the nearby factories and mills. Bruce's father held several low-wage factory jobs, while his mother worked as a secretary.

Springsteen, shown here during a show in 1975, is well known for his electrifying live performances.

The Springsteens often had to struggle, and there were few luxuries. This gave young Bruce a populist perspective—a view of life from the position of the common people—that would influence much of his future work, both lyrically and politically.

Young Bruce

Bruce worshiped Elvis Presley and dreamt of one day being a rock and roll star himself. He later said, "Until I realized that rock music was my connection to the rest of the human race, I felt like I was dying, for some reason, and I didn't really know why." When Bruce saw Elvis appear on *The Ed Sullivan Show* in 1958, he told his mother, "I wanna be just like that." His mother bought him his first guitar, but his father was particularly opposed to Bruce's musical ambitions. Bruce's father felt that young Bruce was uncontrollably rebellious and irresponsible. But Bruce didn't let his father's objections stand in his way. This struggle and disapproval inspired some of

Bruce's most heartfelt songs, such as "Adam Raised a Cain" (1978):

You're born into this life paying
For the sins of somebody else's past
Daddy worked his whole life for nothing but the pain
Now he walks these empty rooms, looking for
something to blame

In 1978, Bruce explained how important music was to him when he was growing up: "Rock and roll, man, it changed my life. It was like *The Voice of America*, the real America, coming into your home. It was the liberating thing, the out. Once I found the guitar, I had the key to the highway." Bruce has always been quick to point out how he was affected by music, even though his father was not always supportive: "Music saved me," he said. "From the beginning, my guitar was something I could go to. If I hadn't found music, I don't know what I would have done."

Defying his father, Bruce joined his first band in the mid-1960s, when he was just sixteen. The band was called the Castiles. They were a five-piece rock band who played mostly Beatles and Rolling Stones covers and some originals at rock clubs in the working-class shore town of Asbury Park, New Jersey. The Castiles also performed at local "battle of the band" competitions, often winning the top spot. They soon developed a following among the Jersey shore's rock-club circuit. The Castiles even recorded a single, written by Bruce and singer George Theiss, called "Baby I" that is a popular request on oldies stations to this day.

By 1968, the Castiles had broken up. But Bruce was still fixated on a musical career.

Fun Fact!

In 1968, Bruce's parents moved to California. Bruce, however, remained in New Jersey, living in the attic of a surfboard factory in Asbury Park! He also briefly attended nearby Ocean County Community College.

13

Bruce on stage with his longtime guitarist, "Little Steven" Van Zandt.

Bruce explained, "Before rock 'n' roll, I didn't have any purpose. I tried to play football and baseball and all those things and I just didn't fit. I was running through a maze. It was never a hobby. It was a reason to live. It was the only one I had. It was kind of life or death." He knew that he wanted to pursue music full-time, so he formed another new band called Earth, based in Asbury Park.

Asbury Park was the place in which Bruce began to develop his loyal fan base, but it was also where he drew much of his inspiration and shaped his developing musical style. Asbury Park was a tourist destination and a local hot spot for nightlife. During this time in Asbury Park, Bruce first met guitarist Steven Van Zandt, who would become a longtime friend and musical collaborator, as well as a star in his own right.

The Boss

The next year, Bruce formed another new band, Child, but the name was soon changed to Steel Mill. Steel Mill was probably Bruce's most famous early band. The musical style of Steel Mill was distinct among the local rock bands, characterized by extended, bluesy instrumental passages, and Bruce's unique, passionate lyrical experimentation. Because of his insistence on three- and four-hour rehearsals, as well as his prominence as the band's frontman, he was known as the Boss. Nicknames were common in this scene, however. The lineup of Steel Mill changed a couple of times, but among the members were guitarist "Miami" Steve Van Zandt, accordionist Danny "Phantom" Federici, and drummer Vini "Mad Dog" Lopez.

Bruce and his friends were eager for success. In 1970, the members of Steel Mill decided to take a road trip to California to see if they could get some attention there. They played a few dates at a club called the Matrix in San Francisco. There was some critical acclaim for Steel Mill among the local music press, but not much came of it. Broke and disappointed, Steel Mill returned home to the East Coast club scene.

However, this trip to California seemed to be a breaking point for Bruce, and at the height of Steel Mill's popularity in 1971—their outdoor gigs were sometimes attended by more than a

Bruce and Steel Mill, featuring Vincent Lopez, Danny Federici, Garry Tallent, and Clarence Clemons

thousand people—Bruce broke up the band after one last show at Asbury Park's Upstage Club. Increasingly frustrated with the way things were going, a restless Bruce spent the rest of the year experimenting with new band formations, the best-known of which is probably Dr. Zoom and the Sonic Boom, which lasted only three days! Finally, he formed the Bruce

The Big Man, Clarence Clemons

Saxophonist and singer Clarence Clemons, known to Springsteen fans as the Big Man, is probably the most popular and beloved of all E Streeters. Audiences call out for Clarence almost as often as they do for the Boss himself!

Born in 1942 in Norfolk, Virginia, Clarence was the son of a Baptist preacher who thought that rock and roll was the "devil's music"! So the talented young Clarence had to wait until he went to college to play the rock and roll he loved so much. (The classically trained Clarence was a music major at Maryland Eastern Shore University.)

Apart from his work with Bruce, Clarence—along with fellow E Streeter, guitarist Steven Van Zandt—was a member of Ringo Starr's All-Starr Band. Clarence had a Top 40 hit in 1985 with "You're a Friend of Mine," a duet with Jackson Browne. Clarence has also played with artists such as Janis Ian, Gary U.S. Bonds, Ian Hunter, Joe Cocker, Todd Rundgren, and Aretha Franklin. Clarence has his own band, Clarence Clemons and the Red Bank Rockers, and the Big Man also played in the band during the Boss's 1999–2000 World Tour.

Clarence Clemons played saxophone and sang for the E Street Band.

Springsteen Band. The Bruce Springsteen Band included many of the musicians who would eventually comprise the now legendary E Street Band, such as Steven Van Zandt, bassist Garry Tallent, keyboard player David Sancious, and saxophone player Clarence Clemons. Bruce and the band were ready to take the next step.

New Jersey

Bruce's home state has always been a source of inspiration for his music and lyrics. Although his career has taken him to many places across the world, he still has a place in his heart for New Jersey. Bruce recalled, "When I was eighteen and playing in this bar in California people would come up to us and say, 'Hey I really dig you guys! Where ya from?' And I'd say New Jersey and they'd just go, 'Yech! Ech!'" New Jersey was not only the place where Bruce felt most comfortable, but it also held the most appeal for him musically: "I tried to live in

Hometown fans at the Meadowlands Arena in New Jersey reach up to the Boss during a show in 1981.

California for a very short time but I soon found out the place held nothing for me. Musically, I preferred what was going on in New Jersey."

Even Bruce's earliest career advice took a stab at his hometown: "People used to tell me that to be a success, I should say I was from

New York City." But Bruce always understood the importance of being true to yourself and not letting others guide or sway you into believing differently than you do. And his fondness for New Jersey has made him a hometown hero.

1965

Bruce forms his first band, the Castiles, a five-piece rock outfit that performs Beatles and Rolling Stones songs and some originals at small clubs on the Jersey shore.

1972

Bruce forms Bruce Springsteen and the E Street Band and they record *Greetings From Asbury Park, N.J.*, Bruce's debut album.

1978

The Darkness Tour, perhaps the most legendary and favorite of Bruce's tours among Springsteen fans, begins in upstate New York.

1980

"Hungry Heart," the first single from the album *The River*, is the band's first top ten hit (it reaches number five).

1984

"Dancing in the Dark" is released as the first single from *Born in the U.S.A.*, and it is an instant hit. By July, *Born in the U.S.A.* is the country's number one album; it stays in the number one spot for seven weeks and in the top ten albums chart for an amazing eighty-five weeks. The Born in the U.S.A. Tour begins.

1985
Bruce wins his first Grammy Award for "Dancing in the Dark." Soon afterward, he participates in the recording of the hunger-relief song "We Are the World."

1993
Bruce records "Streets of Philadelphia," the title track for the film *Philadelphia*.

1999
Bruce is inducted into the Rock and Roll Hall of Fame. The E Street Band joins him onstage to share in the award; later that evening, they perform at the ceremony.

1992
Human Touch and *Lucky Town* are released on the same day, and Bruce assembles a band for a tour. The new band debuts on *Saturday Night Live*, Bruce's first live television performance.

2001
An HBO concert special is filmed, with plans to release the show on video/DVD. Bruce continues to make special, unannounced appearances at New Jersey rock clubs like the Stone Pony.

Hungry Heart

The Bruce Springsteen Band, in various formations and with changing lineups, continued to play local gigs in New Jersey before Bruce broke up that band as well. Bruce decided instead to play some solo gigs in New York City cafés. It was around this time that Bruce met a record producer named Mike

Appel, who soon became his manager. Appel had already enjoyed modest success as a cowriter of pop tunes and was looking for new artists to represent.

"New York City Serenade"

Very eager to get his career off the ground, Bruce quickly signed a management agreement with Mike Appel—a very strict contract that would come back to haunt Bruce later in his career. However, Appel initially helped Bruce land an audition with a Columbia Records executive, John Hammond, who was famous for discovering folk-rock star Bob Dylan. Bruce played a few songs for Hammond in Hammond's office. After hearing him play, Hammond said, "The kid absolutely knocked me out. I only hear somebody really good once every ten years, and not only was Bruce the best, he was a lot better than Dylan when I first heard him." The executive was so impressed with Bruce that he arranged an audition that very night at the Gaslight Club in New York, where Bruce could play for other Columbia hotshots.

Bruce Springsteen's first record, *Greetings from Asbury Park, N.J.*, celebrated life on the Jersey shore.

The Gaslight audition was a big success, and Columbia immediately offered Bruce Springsteen a record contract.

Bruce recorded his debut album, *Greetings From Asbury Park, N.J.*, at the famous CBS Studios in New York. A hastily gathered set of backup musicians (which included old friends Garry Tallent, Vini Lopez, David Sancious, and Clarence Clemons) would be given the nickname the E Street Band, after a sign that hung outside Sancious's home in Belmar, New Jersey. John Hammond himself was at the mixing board. The album was a celebration of Jersey shore street life, with stories about growing up interspersed with piano melodies and horns.

Hitting the Big Time

In January 1973, *Greetings From Asbury Park, N.J.*, was released in the United States. Bruce and the E Street Band toured both the East and West Coasts in support of the new album. They even played some gigs as the opening act for the popular band Chicago. These shows involved playing in extremely large arenas, for tens of thousands of people who were mostly indifferent to Bruce's music, perhaps because

Bruce plays onstage with longtime friend and collaborator Clarence Clemons during a 1978 show.

The E Street Band, circa 1978, included many of Bruce's longtime musical partners, including Van Zandt and Clemons.

he was an unknown. Audience members threw things at the band and showed no interest in their music. Bruce, who was used to the intimacy of small rock clubs and the loyalty of the crowds he played for, found the experience very alienating. He even stated that he would never play another "shed" again, angrily punching a wall. Nevertheless, once he was a star in his own right, Bruce would break that vow and play many arenas just a few years later.

Greetings From Asbury Park, N.J. was getting some attention from rock critics and industry insiders, but sales remained modest. Bruce and the E Street Band quickly recorded a second album, *The Wild, the Innocent & the E Street Shuffle.* It was released in the United States in early November 1973. *The Wild, the Innocent & the E Street Shuffle* was an ambitious album, full of romantic serenades to the boardwalk and old friends. It contained the love song "Rosalita," which would become a signature for Bruce's live performances. But while *The Wild, the Innocent & the E Street Shuffle* received even greater critical acclaim than the first Bruce Springsteen album, it still didn't sell very well. Bruce and the band decided to embark on another round of touring to hopefully drum up some interest in the new record.

33

"I Saw Rock and Roll Future"

Despite sluggish record sales, underground attention to Bruce Springsteen and the E Street Band's records was building. The spectacular, athletic live shows, which typically lasted for hours, were where Bruce received the most serious attention. After seeing a Bruce Springsteen show on May 9, 1974, at Harvard Square Theatre in Cambridge, Massachusetts, legendary rock critic Jon Landau uttered this famous line: "I saw rock and roll future, and its name is Bruce Springsteen." After Landau published this statement in an essay, Bruce and Landau became close friends. Later, after a long legal battle, Landau became Bruce's manager. The article's famous quote was also used in a future Bruce Springsteen promotional campaign.

The sessions for Bruce's third album, *Born to Run,* began in the spring and summer of 1975 at the Record Plant in New York. During the sessions, Bruce's new friend and manager, Jon Landau, took on an increasingly bigger role as producer—at former manager Mike Appel's expense. In July 1975, the *Born to Run* tour began, six weeks prior to the album's release. This became a regular practice for the tour-loving Bruce: to begin playing live shows, and offering new material to loyal fans, before albums were released for sale. In August, Bruce Springsteen and the E Street Band performed perhaps the most important shows of their career during a five-night gig at the Bottom Line in New York City. The shows were attended by various important industry people, and one show was even broadcast on the radio. During these performances, Bruce greatly impressed many important people in the music industry and the music press, and they helped turn him into a rock superstar.

Born to Run

Born to Run was released on September 1, 1975. It is a landmark album that landed Springsteen simultaneously on the covers of *Time* and *Newsweek* in the last week of October 1975. Bruce was proud of his efforts and especially the title song: "I wanted 'Born to Run' to be a hit single.

Not for the bucks but because I really believed in the song a whole lot and I just wanted to hear it on the radio, on AM across the country. For me, that's where a song should be."

Bruce's celebrity and popularity were skyrocketing. In late November, Bruce and the band began their first-ever European tour, playing four shows in three cities. Embarrassed and confused by his newfound fame, a Bruce Springsteen legend has it that before the first of these shows, he ran through the concert hall, tearing down posters that read "Finally, London is ready for Bruce Springsteen." After this leg of the tour, Bruce and the band returned to the United States, wrapping up the year with a New Year's Eve show at the Tower Theater in Philadelphia.

As 1976 began, Bruce once again hit the road on what was called the Chicken Scratch Tour, playing small venues in such southern towns as Durham, North Carolina; Auburn, Alabama; and Shreveport, Louisiana. After Chicken Scratch was over, Bruce began a legal battle with Mike Appel. He wanted to break his management contract with Appel and have more control over his income and, most important, retain the rights to his songs. Furthermore, Bruce wanted Jon Landau to be the producer of his future albums. After being sued by Bruce, Appel countersued for fraud, saying that Bruce had broken an agreement he had put in writing. Appel's countersuit was also an attempt to keep Bruce from recording with Landau.

New Producer, New Album

Unable to record new music, Bruce spent the rest of 1976 touring with the band and making guest appearances with punk poet Patti Smith, fellow New Jersey–based rock and roller Southside Johnny, and others. The lawsuits kept Bruce from recording any new material for more than two years. Finally, on May 28, 1977, Bruce and Mike Appel made an out-of-court settlement that gave Bruce full control of his music. When Bruce was at last able to reenter the studio, Landau was his producer as well as his manager. Springsteen finally had total control of his song catalog and his career. Immediately, on

Steven Van Zandt

Steven Van Zandt has had an exceptional and varied career in the music business for more than twenty-five years. He is a distinguished and sought-after record producer, overseeing the recording of albums for artists as notable and eclectic as Bruce Springsteen, Southside Johnny and the Asbury Jukes, rock-soul powerhouse Darlene Love, Gary U.S. Bonds, Michael Monroe (former lead singer of glam-metal band Hanoi Rocks), and the Lords of the New Church (featuring the late Stiv Bators, lead singer of punk rock's beloved Dead Boys). Steven has written songs for many artists, including reggae legend Jimmy Cliff and former Stray Cat Brian Setzer. He has led his own band, Little Steven and the Disciples of Soul, in addition to being a prominent member of the E Street Band and Southside Johnny's Asbury Jukes. Steven is often credited for developing what is now known as the Asbury Park Sound: bluesy, horn-driven rock and roll music.

A committed political activist, in the early 1980s, Steven founded Artists United Against Apartheid, a human rights project best known for spawning the multi-artist smash hit "Sun City." The *Sun City* album was cited by *Rolling Stone* magazine as one of the 100 best albums

The multitalented Steven Van Zandt has had success as a musician, actor, and activist.

of the 1980s, and Steven was given the International Documentary Association Award for his film *The Making of Sun City*. In 1985, Steven established the Solidarity Foundation to support the rights of native peoples to govern their own lands. He has been honored twice by the United Nations for his efforts in support of human rights.

Today, Steven enjoys a whole new type of fame—as a TV star on the HBO series *The Sopranos*, in which he portrays a mobster, Silvio Dante. "Affection," one of the songs that plays over the show's closing credits, is by Steven's latest band, the Lost Boys. Lost Boys songs are also included on *The Sopranos* sound track CD.

The album *Darkness on the Edge of Town* was a dark, raw, and personal record for Bruce.

June 1, Bruce entered a New York studio to begin the recording of his next album, which would be known as *Darkness on the Edge of Town*. The resulting album was dark, almost bleak, and critics hailed Bruce's raw, emotional expressions. Much of it seemed inspired by his troubled relationship with the past, with songs such as "Factory" addressing his father's tough working life.

"I'm a Rocker"

A tour to support the new album began in Buffalo, New York, in May 1978. To this day, the Darkness Tour is considered the most legendary of all of Bruce's tours by

Fun Fact!

In late April 1976, after a show in Memphis, Tennessee, Bruce and Steven Van Zandt took a cab to Elvis Presley's estate, Graceland. Bruce climbed over the wall and attempted to meet his hero, Elvis—this was a year before Presley died—but was soon booted out by a Graceland guard!

Bruce loyalists. Bruce seemed to pour his entire life into every sweaty, exuberant performance. During the tour, in late August, Bruce appeared on the cover of *Rolling Stone* for the first—but far from last—time. The Darkness Tour ended with a marathon show in Cleveland, Ohio, on the first day of

The Boss at an antinuclear benefit at New York's Madison Square Garden

1979. Despite the fact that a firecracker, thrown by a crazed audience member, exploded in Bruce's face, the show was Bruce's longest ever, with more than thirty songs played. But he would top even that record by the next tour.

In April 1979, Bruce again entered the studio with the E Street Band, this time to record what became *The River*. On a motorcycle trip, Bruce crashed into a tree and injured his leg, forcing him to stay in bed for three weeks. The accident spawned a rumor that Bruce had been killed!

In the fall, Bruce and the band joined a host of other artists, including crooner Jackson Browne, funk diva Chaka Khan, blues singer Bonnie Raitt, and rock and roller Tom Petty, for two antinuclear benefit shows at Madison Square Garden in New York, known as the No Nukes shows. Bruce did a ninety-minute set each night and debuted the song "The River." The second night also happened to be his thirtieth birthday. Some of the songs from Bruce's performances were later used for the No Nukes album and movie. *The River* sessions dragged on and on into the fall and winter.

It's Hard to Be a Saint in the City

By September 1980, the recordings for *The River*, which had been going on throughout the year, finally ended. More than sixty songs had been finished. The very next month, the River Tour began in Ann Arbor, Michigan, and as was typical for Bruce, the album had not even been released yet. The tour was characterized by astonishingly long shows that typically included more than thirty songs and lasted well over three hours— sometimes almost four.

Finally released in October 1980, *The River* was a two-record set that was Bruce's first number one album, and it made him an international superstar. On New Year's Eve, Bruce and the band ended a three-night stand at Nassau Coliseum in New York with a New Year's Eve show that still ranks as the longest set Bruce has ever played, lasting more than four hours and containing almost forty songs!

"Working on the Highway"

In 1981, a planned spring European tour was postponed slightly because of exhaustion on the part of the constantly touring Bruce. But by April, it finally kicked off in Hamburg, Germany. This was the first full-scale tour for Bruce and the band outside of North America. The tour included thirty-three shows in ten countries. Sixteen of these shows were played in England, most at Wembley Arena in London. Perhaps to avoid another bout of exhaustion, the shows were now considerably shorter than they were the year before and remained so for the rest of the tour.

After returning home from Europe in June, Bruce and the E Street Band continued touring by christening the newly built Meadowlands Arena in East Rutherford, New Jersey, with a six-night stand in early July. On August 20, one of the

Fun Fact!

Bruce originally wrote "Hungry Heart" for the legendary punk rock band the Ramones. When his manager heard the song, however, he convinced Bruce to keep it for himself. Luckily, he listened—"Hungry Heart" was Bruce's first top ten hit!

best and most famous shows of Bruce's career took place at the Sports Arena in Los Angeles. It was a benefit for the Vietnam Veterans of America (VVA), and it turned into a passionate platform for some of Bruce's beliefs. Onstage, he said: "It's like when you're walking down a dark street late at night, and out of the corner of your eye you see somebody getting hurt . . . but you keep walking because you think it don't have nothing to do with you . . . Vietnam turned the whole country into that dark street, and unless we walk down those dark alleys and look into the eyes of those men and women, we're never gonna get home." Over $100,000 was raised for VVA at the event.

Back to Basics

This time marked a significant turning point for Bruce Springsteen and the E Street Band. The band had played for full arenas practically everywhere, and Bruce had established himself as one of the hardest-working and most exciting live performers in the world. According to Bruce, this was also the first time in his life when money was no longer a problem; he was on his way to becoming quite wealthy. The River Tour ended in Cincinnati, Ohio, in September 1981. This was also Steven Van Zandt's last show as an official member of the E Street Band until 1999; he was replaced by guitarist Nils Lofgren.

By 1982, perhaps feeling wearied by the trappings of fame and success, Bruce decided to again revisit his working-class roots. In the bedroom of his new home in Holmdel, New Jersey, Bruce started off the year by recording new songs on a four-track tape recorder. In April, he entered a studio, using the songs he recorded alone at home as demos, but only a few of them worked out satisfactory with band members. Bruce decided to record the new album's songs the way he had originally created them: by himself.

A New Kind of Success

The result was *Nebraska*. Released in October 1983, its bleak, all-acoustic lyricism was hardly radio-friendly, but it still reached number three on the charts. In December, Bruce's first real (non-concert) music video premiered on MTV. The chosen song was "Atlantic City." Bruce himself does not appear in the video. It is a grainy, black-and-white video that matches the song, a downbeat tune about the disenfranchised in America:

Now, I been lookin' for a job, but it's hard to find
Down here it's just winners and losers and don't get
caught on the wrong side of that line
Well, I'm tired of comin' out on the losin' end
So, honey, last night I met this guy and I'm gonna do
a little favor for him.

To this day, the song is considered one of Springsteen's best—and saddest.

In 1984, Bruce and the band immediately began to work on a new album. For his next record, Bruce was ready to make a rock and roll blockbuster. That summer, at the same time that Bruce was recording, he made a record number of surprise guest appearances with various bands at Jersey shore bars. Sometimes he played several times a week with local artists—sometimes twice in one day! Most of these gigs took place at the Stone Pony in Asbury Park. The unannounced club performances continued for the rest of the year.

BORN IN THE U.S.A./BRUCE SPRINGSTEEN

In 1984, Bruce and the E Street Band released *Born in the U.S.A.*, which made Bruce into one of the biggest rock stars in the world.

"Between Heaven and Earth"

When Bruce and the band were finally finished recording, the result was *Born in the U.S.A.* The

album went on to become one of the biggest-
selling records in history, and launched seven
top-ten singles, including the title song. The first
single, "Dancing in the Dark," was released on
May 9 to promote the album, due for release on
June 4. *Born in the U.S.A.* was Bruce's most
commercial album to date. For many music fans
(as well as many casual listeners of commercial
radio) the first exposure to Bruce Springsteen
was the "Dancing in the Dark" single and video.
Sure enough, the song was a tremendous success,
thanks in no small part to the charming video,
which features Bruce in concert, pulling an
excited young fan onstage with him to dance.
The Bruce fan in the video became TV superstar
Courteney Cox-Arquette, best known as Monica
from the long-running NBC hit *Friends.*

   Born in the U.S.A. went to number one on the
Billboard chart the first week of July 1984. The
record was nothing short of a phenomenon; it
stayed in the top spot for seven weeks and in the
top ten for an incredible eighty-five weeks. In late
July, the Born in the U.S.A. Tour began in St. Paul,
Minnesota. The band had also grown with backup

singer and New Jersey native Patti Scialfa. Ten shows at the Meadowlands in New Jersey marked the homecoming of the Born in the U.S.A. Tour. The shows were sold out in a matter of hours, as were all the other shows on the tour. The last of the ten Jersey shows, a thirty-three-song, four-hour marathon, was further fueled in intensity by the appearance of E Street legend Steven Van Zandt.

Presidential Mention

On September 19, 1984, while campaigning for reelection in Hammonton, New Jersey, conservative United States president Ronald Reagan mentioned Bruce Springsteen in a campaign speech. Reportedly, the president said, "America's future lies in a thousand dreams inside your hearts. It rests in the message of hope in songs of a man so many Americans admire: New Jersey's own Bruce Springsteen. And helping you make those dreams come true is what this job of mine is all about."

It was the first time that any president had cited the work of a rock star in a campaign speech, but this hardly made it an honor. Bruce's politics had little in common with Reagan's, as the president had dismantled programs to benefit the poor and homeless while unemployment and inflation rates soared. Bruce resented the way that Reagan was trying to capitalize on Bruce's "everyman" appeal. Almost immediately, Bruce made a pointed, but humorous, reply from a concert stage in Pittsburgh. "The president mentioned my name the other day," he said. "I kinda got to wondering what his favorite album must be. I don't think it was *Nebraska*." From that point forth, Bruce began to support local food banks, shelters, and other social organizations that worked on behalf of the poor and homeless, wherever the tour brought the band.

Keeping Busy

Bruce and the band toured the United States and Canada for the rest of 1984. In January 1985, "Dancing in the Dark" won Bruce his first Grammy Award for best pop/rock single, but he was not in attendance at the Grammy ceremony. Later in January, Bruce participated in the

"We Are the World" recording session. "We Are the World" was a joint effort between Michael Jackson and producer Quincy Jones to create a charity record. Many popular musicians, such as Stevie Wonder, Tina Turner, and Billy Joel, were in attendance to record the song. Bruce, eager to donate his time to charitable causes, was also there to help record "We Are the World." The song raised over $50 million and the proceeds were donated to aid African hunger relief.

In March, Bruce and the band performed their inaugural show in Brisbane, Australia; the show, the first of eight, was the band's first real outdoor stadium show. In April, the band headed to Tokyo for their first shows in Japan. They played eight shows there as well. Briefly back in the States again, Bruce married model-actress Julianne Philips in a private ceremony in Oregon in May of 1985. Afterward, Bruce quickly returned to the European leg of the tour, which began at Slane Castle in Dublin, Ireland, in June. More than 100,000 people attended, and it is reported that Bruce had to frequently stop the show to calm down fans suffering from "Brucemania"! On July 4,

In 1985, along with countless other rock and pop stars, Bruce helped record "We Are the World," a benefit song for famine relief in Africa.

the band performed the first of three shows, for over 70,000 people at a time, at London's enormous Wembley Stadium. The show opened with an acoustic version of "Independence Day" and was later honored with another surprise appearance from Steven Van Zandt, who had by then become a solo artist known as Little Steven.

The final leg of the Born in the U.S.A. Tour was a stretch of stadium shows in the United States, beginning in Washington, D.C., in August. Bruce played eight shows at New Jersey's Meadowlands, each attended by sold-out crowds of more than 80,000 people! The Born in the U.S.A. Tour ended in late September with four shows at the Memorial Coliseum in Los Angeles. The last one featured an hour-long set of encores and closed with "Glory Days." The fifteen-month tour was, from start to finish, a special professional triumph for Bruce, establishing him as the biggest music superstar in the world, perhaps rivaled only by Michael Jackson or Madonna.

"Blood Brothers"

At the end of July 1985, Bruce lent his voice to another protest record, this time Little Steven's anti-apartheid song, "Sun City." Apartheid was the official policy of segregation and political and economic discrimination against black people in South Africa by the white South African government; it was abolished in 1990. The song,

57

Bruce sings "Born in the U.S.A." in front of a sold-out crowd in Washington, D.C., during the kickoff show of his 1985 tour.

Nils Lofgren

Talented and sought-after E Street guitarist Nils Lofgren is undoubtedly a legend in his own right. Born in 1951, Nils became a professional musician at just seventeen, when he joined blues-rocker Neil Young's band. Nils sang and played piano and guitar on the platinum Neil Young album *After the Gold Rush* (1970), as well as *Tonight's the Night* (1973). After recording several albums with the band Grin in the early 1970s, Nils went solo in 1975 with a self-titled debut. Another album, *Cry Tough*, was released in 1976 and was followed by a worldwide tour.

Four more critically acclaimed solo albums followed, as did another stint with Neil Young in the early 1980s. Finally, in 1984, the multitalented Nils joined Springsteen's E Street Band, replacing Steven Van Zandt. Nils played more than 150 shows worldwide on the Born in the U.S.A. Tour. He was also a studio musician for the *Tunnel of Love* album, and he played on the subsequent tour as well as on the Amnesty International tour. Nils has also been in several of Bruce

Springsteen's videos, including "Dancing in the Dark" and "Glory Days."

Nils released his most successful solo record, *Flip*, in 1985. Afterward, he toured with former Beatle Ringo Starr's All-Starr Band. In

Nils jams onstage with Bruce during a show in New Jersey.

1992, the All-Starr Band, including Nils, went on a second world tour and released another live album in 1993. Four more Nils Lofgren solo records followed, as did an appearance with Neil Young on Young's *MTV Unplugged* special. The *Neil Young Unplugged* CD went platinum.

To this day, Lofgren continues to be in demand as a studio musician, working with artists as diverse as Branford Marsalis and Cab Calloway. He has served as the musical director for the CableAce Awards and participated in various tours, including the 1999–2000 World Tour with Bruce Springsteen and the E Street Band. Most recently, Nils's song "Black Books" was featured on the HBO hit show *The Sopranos*—starring his fellow E Streeter, Steven Van Zandt!

recorded under the name Artists United Against Apartheid, featured many other legendary music stars, including Pat Benatar, Bono, Jimmy Cliff, George Clinton, Miles Davis, Bob Dylan, Bonnie Raitt, Joey Ramone, Lou Reed, Gil Scott-Heron, and Pete Townsend. These artists came together to educate the public about Sun City and apartheid in South Africa. They sang about their decision to no longer perform in Sun City.

At the beginning of 1986, Bruce was once again chosen as Artist of the Year in a *Rolling Stone* annual poll, and he won the top spot in just about every album and song category as well. Later that month, on January 19, Bruce returned to the stage when he and most of the E Street Band performed a benefit for the 3M plant in Freehold, New Jersey, which was about to be shut down.

For his next project, Bruce had his sights set on a live album, and he spent most of the spring and summer selecting and mixing songs for it. He took a night out to play his first live acoustic gig since 1972, at Neil Young's Bridge School benefit show on October 13. Neil Young and his wife, Pegi, cofounded the Bridge School in 1986 for children with severe physical and speech impairments; their son, Ben, was one of the school's first students. Bruce was joined at the Bridge School benefit show by accordionist Danny Federici and guitarist Nils Lofgren. This event was also the first time that "Born in the U.S.A." was performed outside the studio in its original acoustic-blues style arrangement, the way it was originally created during the *Nebraska* sessions.

The Promised Land

4

In 1986, Bruce was having a good time selecting and mixing songs for the planned live album set, *Bruce Springsteen & the E Street Band Live/1975–85*. But while this was undoubtedly the peak of his commercial success, Bruce's personal life was somewhat troubled. The pressures of international stardom were taking their toll on Bruce and his wife, Julianne Phillips, who were constantly hounded by paparazzi, or members of the press. This, combined with Bruce's workaholic nature and Julianne's rising stardom, caused turbulence in the young marriage.

Bruce Springsteen & the E Street Band Live/1975–85 hit the stores in November 1986. The five-album box set covered almost all of Bruce's career up to that point, and the expectations for the album's success were enormous. Sure enough, it sold three million copies upon release and was soon catapulted to the top spot on *Billboard's* album chart, an unprecedented feat for a multi-record set. The limits of Bruce's accomplishments seemed to be infinite. In 1987, for the third time in a row, Bruce was elected Artist of the Year in the *Rolling Stone* poll. On January 21, Bruce inducted Roy Orbison into the Rock and Roll Hall of Fame.

That spring through summer, Bruce worked on a follow-up album to *Born in the U.S.A.* in his home studio in Rumson, New Jersey. Most of the time he worked by himself, and although members of the E Street Band made appearances throughout the sessions, at no time was the entire band reunited in the studio. Bruce seemed to be going through a very introverted, contemplative period. The result was *Tunnel of Love,* a confessional album that won the number twenty-five spot in *Rolling Stone* magazine's 100 best LPs of the '80s survey.

Bruce's popularity made many fans curious about his private life. Bruce's wife, Julianne Phillips, was pulled into the spotlight with him.

Julianne Phillips

Legend has it that Bruce Springsteen spotted model Julianne Phillips in a fashion magazine and called her up for a date. Bruce and Julianne had a whirlwind romance and married in May 1985. At the time, some fans criticized Bruce for the marriage, which they saw as a superficial, disappointing rock star–model pairing.

Problems quickly developed in the Springsteen-Phillips marriage; many of the songs on Bruce's *Tunnel of Love* are thought to be commentary on the troubled relationship. Sure enough, the couple divorced in 1989, the same year it was reported that Bruce was having an affair with E Street Band backup singer Patti Scialfa (whom he later married, in 1991). By most reports, Bruce and Julianne's divorce was amicable, although Julianne reportedly was asked to sign an agreement that she would not speak publicly about her marriage to Bruce or write a tell-all book.

Julianne Phillips, whom Bruce married in 1985 and divorced in 1989

"When You're Alone"

Tunnel of Love was released in October 1987. The album was a drastic turnaround for Bruce. While he could have easily made a predictable, commercial record that sounded just like *Born in the U.S.A.*, he instead chose twelve reflective, mournful songs, mostly about love and relationships. Some critics believed that the album, which hinted at marital problems, was

Did You Know?

Julianne Phillips occasionally appears in TV movies and feature films. She is probably best known for her role as Frankie on the popular NBC television series *Sisters*, which ran for several years in the early 1990s.

a love letter to his wife, Julianne. The mature-sounding album disappointed many longtime fans and sold far fewer copies than the phenomenal *Born in the U.S.A.* Nonetheless, *Tunnel of Love* went double platinum on its first day of release, and three weeks after release it was number one on the charts. Rumors about a *Tunnel of Love* tour swirled around for the rest of the year. At one point, Bruce even considered playing a small-scale acoustic tour—solo, without the E Street Band.

The next year began much like many before it. On January 20, 1988, Bruce inducted folk-rock

Patti Scialfa

Patti Scialfa is a longstanding member of the E Street Band and also is a talented singer, songwriter, and guitarist in her own right. Patti, a native of Deal, New Jersey, joined the E Street Band for the 1984 tour to support *Born in the U.S.A.* Even before joining the E Street Band, Patti was already well known on the Jersey shore music scene, playing with popular bands such as Southside Johnny and the Asbury Jukes.

While singing background vocals for *Tunnel of Love*, the turbulent and often sad album that chronicled Bruce's marital troubles with Julianne Phillips, a relationship began between Patti and Bruce. Julianne filed for a divorce soon after the affair became public in the tabloids, and Bruce and Patti began a legendary rock and roll romance.

Patti has also contributed vocals to Bruce's albums *Human Touch* and *Lucky Town*. In 1993, her eagerly awaited solo effort, *Rumble Doll*, was released. Patti wrote or cowrote all the tracks on *Rumble Doll*, and the record was praised by critics. Patti was also part of the reunited E Street Band for the 1999–2000 Springsteen World Tour.

legend Bob Dylan into the Rock and Roll Hall of Fame. The next month, the Tunnel of Love Express Tour began in Worcester, Massachusetts. The tour not only included the E Street Band but also a horn section. The tour rolled through the United States with mostly indoor shows at big arenas during the rest of the spring and early summer. It continued in Europe; the first show

Bruce takes the stage with Bob Dylan during a performance at the Rock and Roll Hall of Fame in 1995.

The Stone Pony

The Stone Pony is one of the world's most well known and legendary rock and roll venues, rivaling Los Angeles's Whiskey and New York's CBGB in status. Rock and Roll Hall of Fame Vice President Robert Santelli called the Pony "one of the greatest rock clubs of all time." Rock fans from around the world make special pilgrimages to Asbury Park, New Jersey, just to catch a show at the Stone Pony.

The Stone Pony opened in 1974, and since that time innumerable artists—including Jon Bon Jovi, Patti Smith, the Smithereens, the Kinks, Elvis Costello, Joan Jett, and the Pretenders—have taken the stage. The club was renovated in 2000, preserving its original character and adding an exhibition of nostalgic Asbury Park and Stone Pony art and artifacts.

A beloved local landmark, the Stone Pony regularly hosts community events, both charitable and artistic, including photography exhibits, benefits for local and world hunger, and fund-raising events for the Jersey Shore Jazz & Blues Foundation. The club is even an official drop-off location for the food banks of Monmouth and Ocean Counties. Also, the Stone Pony Foundation was established to fund music education for elementary and high school students.

Asbury Park, N.J.'s Stone Pony is a world-famous rock venue.

was in Italy. It was during the band's stay in Rome that a paparazzi photographer got a shot of Bruce and E Street Band backup vocalist Patti Scialfa sharing a romantic moment—both wearing only underpants! The picture confirmed what had been a regular rumor since the beginning of the tour: Longtime friends and musical collaborators Bruce and Patti were having a love affair.

Around the World

On June 18, 1988, Bruce performed four acoustic songs at an antiracist benefit in Paris, accompanied only by E Street Band saxophonist Clarence Clemons. In July, and for the first time in his career, Bruce played a show behind the Iron Curtain, in East Berlin, Germany. The Iron Curtain had literally walled off East Germany from West Germany, isolating the former under Soviet control. This show also marked Bruce's largest audience to date—nearly 180,000 people.

The Tunnel of Love Express Tour ended in August in Barcelona, Spain. Rumors surfaced that Bruce would play his usual set of shows in New Jersey, but this never occurred, disappointing loyal fans. In fact, the Tunnel of Love Express Tour was the first in which Bruce didn't play his home state. Even more troubling for Bruce Springsteen loyalists, the tour was also the last major tour that would feature the E Street Band (until 1999). Not only that, but the Tunnel of Love Express shows had been characterized by fixed set lists and rigid, nearly staged performances and onstage banter— a stark departure from the athletic, boisterous, exciting attitude fans had come to expect from Bruce. However, as the Tunnel of Love Express Tour progressed, Bruce played fewer new songs (and obscure old songs) and began to incorporate recent hits that had proved to be crowd pleasers.

"Living Proof"

Bruce also took some time out to support worthy causes. In early September, the Human Rights

Bruce, shown here with *(from left)* U2's Bono, Tracy Chapman, and Sting, was one of countless artists on Amnesty International's Human Rights Now! Tour.

Now! Tour began, its first show at Wembley Stadium in London. The year 1988 marked the fortieth anniversary of the Universal Declaration of Human Rights, a document signed by nearly every government in the world to recognize the existence of inalienable human rights, regardless of race, sex, religion, or political opinion. The Human Rights Now! Tour was organized by Amnesty International to celebrate the achievements of the human rights movement and to revive the ideals of basic human rights protection. Hundreds of thousands of people attended sold-out shows across the globe.

Apart from Bruce Springsteen, the Human Rights Now! lineup included Sting, Peter Gabriel, Tracy Chapman, and world music superstar Youssour N'Dour. Bruce and the E Street Band closed the show with an hour-and-a-half set, as they would do at every stop on the tour. The Human Rights Now! Tour continued across the world, with shows in Europe, Africa, Asia, North America, and South America. The tour ended with a huge show in Buenos Aires, Argentina. This performance would mark the last announced live performance of the E Street Band until 1999. (Bruce, however, would play another Amnesty International show ten years later in 1998, on the fiftieth anniversary of the Universal Declaration of Human Rights, with a solo acoustic performance in Paris, France, on December 10.)

Bruce and Julianne's divorce became official on March 1, 1989. Bruce worked out his heartbreak with another club-hopping summer, performing unannounced sets, to the surprised delight of local rock fans, at Jersey shore bars on numerous occasions. On September 23, Bruce celebrated his fortieth birthday at the Stone Pony in Asbury Park, where he danced with his mother and performed with most of the E Street Band.

But the very next month, Bruce called each member of the E Street Band and told them that he would be working with other musicians for his next album and that they should feel free to pursue other projects. This act was considered the official breakup of Bruce Springsteen and the E Street Band.

No Surrender

As always, Bruce started the new year, 1991, by working on a new album, which he wanted to call *Human Touch*. In April, Bruce and Patti Scialfa moved into a Beverly Hills mansion, causing a bit of talk among fans who feared the Boss was going Hollywood. A few months earlier, Bruce and Patti had their first child, a baby boy named Evan James. On June 8, 1991, Bruce and Patti were married, and on December 30, 1991, their second child, Jessica Rae, was born. The birth was announced by Steven Van Zandt to millions of television viewers during Little Steven's New Year's Eve performance at Times Square in New York City.

By the end of the year, the *Human Touch* album was basically finished and ready for a December release. But suddenly, Bruce hit a productive streak and decided to continue recording. What resulted from this creative outpouring would become the *Lucky Town* album.

The New Band

Human Touch and *Lucky Town* were released on the same day, March 31, 1992. In April, Bruce began the work of assembling a new touring band. It would eventually consist of Roy Bittan (keyboards), Shane Fontayne (guitar), Tommy Sims (bass), Zachary Alford (drums), and singers Bobby King, Crystal Taliefero, Carol Dennis, Angel Rogers, Cleo Kennedy, Gia Ciambotti, and sometimes Patti Scialfa. The new band played its first gig almost exclusively for Sony executives at the Bottom Line in New York

Patti Scialfa and the Boss in New York in 2001

on May 6. A few days later, the band made its first public debut on *Saturday Night Live*, which also marked Bruce's first live television appearance.

Bruce began another round of touring, and this would be his first world tour in nearly four years. It began in mid-June in Stockholm, Sweden, under extreme media scrutiny. A nervous band made it through the three-hour show, but the reception from the audience was mixed—many fans wanted to hear old favorites, not new songs. For instance, "Born to Run" was not played for the first time since 1975, and this upset some people, who clearly came to see Bruce perform his most famous tunes. But a few days later, Bruce sang the song in Milan, Italy, and made sure to play it for the rest of the tour's gigs.

In July and August, Bruce was back in New Jersey for his first shows there since 1985—eleven in all. But Bruce continued to play new songs and revive rare older ones at the expense of surefire crowd pleasers, satisfying loyal fans at the risk of alienating new ones. The tour continued through October, once again with heavy emphasis on the material from the new albums—despite the fact that they had fallen from *Billboard*'s Top 200 and were considered commercial disappointments. The North American tour ended in Lexington, Kentucky, in December.

A Glimpse into the Future

On January 13, 1993, Bruce inducted Creedence Clearwater Revival into the Rock and Roll Hall of Fame and performed with CCR frontman John Fogerty. On March 23, an acoustic rehearsal show in Red Bank, New Jersey, for some planned European dates with the new band became an unexpected turning point. Bruce not only played songs he hadn't played for almost twenty years, but he also included unrecorded songs from his vast, unreleased catalog. The session seemed to indicate where Bruce was headed for the future.

At the end of that month, a European tour began in Glasgow, Scotland. The tour ended in June in Norway. To complete the tour, Bruce played two benefit shows, called the Concert to Fight Hunger, in New Jersey and New York City. The show at the Meadowlands in New Jersey became a four-hour spectacle with numerous guest stars and musical surprises, such as Clarence Clemons, Max Weinberg, Steven Van Zandt, and Roy Bittan, sparking hope among fans that the E Street Band might reunite. Later that month, Bruce made his first appearance on *Late Night with David Letterman*, playing "Glory Days" with Paul Schafer's band.

"Book of Dreams"

Bruce basically took the rest of the year off to spend time with his family, but he did record one

Did You Know?

In February 1986, Bruce turned down a $12 million offer from Chrysler president Lee Iaccoca to use "Born in the U.S.A." in a commercial, proving once again that he was an independent thinker and artist, and that he could not be bought.

new song in his home studio at the request of movie director Jonathan Demme. Demme wanted Bruce to write the theme song for his new movie, *Philadelphia,* starring Tom Hanks as a man dying from AIDS. Bruce created the melancholy "Streets of Philadelphia," which would eventually be his biggest hit of the decade. Bruce explained his feelings about the project: "The bonus I got out of writing 'Streets of Philadelphia' was that all of a sudden I could go out and meet some gay man somewhere and he wouldn't be afraid to talk to me and say, 'Hey, that song really meant something to me.' My image had always been very heterosexual, very straight. So it was a nice experience for me, a chance to clarify my own feelings about gay and lesbian civil rights."

The beginning of 1994 was a great time for Bruce. On January 5, Bruce and Patti's third child, Sam Ryan, was born. On January 19, Bruce sang "Come Together" with Axl Rose of Guns N' Roses at the Rock and Roll Hall of Fame. And on January 23, Bruce won a Golden Globe Award for "Streets of Philadelphia."

In March, Bruce won an Oscar for "Streets of Philadelphia" and performed the song live with members of his 1992–1993 touring band. Springsteen also won four Grammy Awards for the song in February. "Streets of Philadelphia" won yet another award in September, this time for best song from a movie at MTV's Video Music Awards, and he performed the song live there as well.

Bruce decided to first release a greatest hits compilation instead of a new album, and quickly called in the E Street Band to work on some bonus tracks. The band gathered at the Hit Factory in New York—the first time they were all in the same recording studio at once since 1984. The session was filmed, and footage would later be released as a video entitled *Blood Brothers.* The greatest hits session ended in January 1995, the album was released on February 28, and by March 18, *Greatest Hits* debuted on *Billboard's* chart at number one.

New Directions

In May, Bruce started working on an acoustic folk album, which would be finished by August. The E Street Band was once again briefly reunited in early September at the opening of the Rock and Roll Hall of Fame museum in Cleveland, Ohio. Despite strong rumors of a tour in support of *Greatest Hits*, this is the last time the band was together until 1999. In late October, Bruce once again performed at Neil Young's acoustic Bridge School benefit. He took the opportunity to debut two songs from his upcoming acoustic album.

Springsteen takes the stage with rock and roll legend Chuck Berry at the Rock and Roll Hall of Fame in 1995.

In November 1995, the album *The Ghost of Tom Joad* was released. *The Ghost of Tom Joad* is an album much like *Nebraska.* It chronicles the lives and pain of society's outcasts. On the same day *The Ghost of Tom Joad* was released, Bruce set out on a solo acoustic-folk tour and planned to play in small theaters and intimate clubs for nearly two years. The tour began in New Brunswick, New Jersey, and would continue for the rest of the year in selected American cities. In the beginning of the tour, Bruce's shows were almost gloomy, concentrating nearly exclusively on the downbeat new material and completely ignoring the old favorites.

The tour continued through 1996 in the United States, Canada, and Europe. Two new movies featured Bruce's songs: Sean Penn's *The Crossing Guard* included the track "Missing," while Tim Robbins's *Dead Man Walking* featured a song with that movie's title, taken from the *Tom Joad* album. Bruce interrupted his European tour to go back to the States and perform "Dead Man Walking" at the Oscars on March 25. The song, though nominated, did not win the Oscar. *The Ghost of Tom Joad* won the Grammy for Best Contemporary Folk Album the next year, and its song "Dead Man Walking" earned a nomination for Best Male Rock Vocal Performance.

"Man at the Top"

On November 8, Bruce played a benefit show at his old high school in Freehold, New Jersey.

89

The Boss performed the somber title song from the film *Dead Man Walking* at the sixty-eighth annual Academy Awards in March 1996.

The show was just for Freehold residents, and during it Bruce premiered a song called "Freehold," a sentimental and upbeat number that celebrated Bruce's early stomping grounds.

On May 5, 1997, after a few acoustic tour dates in Japan and Australia, Bruce received the Polar Music Prize. This is a Swedish award that is considered among the finest music awards in the world. It is an international honor awarded to artists or institutions in recognition of exceptional achievements in the world of music. King Carl XVI Gustav of Sweden bestowed Bruce with the prize, and Bruce performed two songs at the official dinner that evening. In May, Bruce performed in Poland for the first time, with two shows in Warsaw. And later that month, he performed in Prague, the capital of the Czech Republic, also for the first time, where he met with Czech president and Bruce Springsteen fan Vaclev Havel.

The tour ended in late May with two shows in Paris. On September 4, Bruce performed at the MTV Video Music Awards with the Wallflowers, whose lead singer, Jakob Dylan, is Bob Dylan's

King Carl Gustav of Sweden presents Bruce with the Polar Music Prize in 1997.

son. And on December 7, Bruce performed Bob Dylan's "The Times They Are A-Changing" at the Kennedy Center Honors in tribute to Dylan, with notable public figures such as President Bill Clinton in attendance. Bruce Springsteen could now fairly be considered a member of the cultural elite.

Glory Days

In late 1997, Bruce Springsteen attended his thirtieth high school reunion with his wife, Patti, in Tinton Falls, New Jersey. It was the first reunion he had ever attended, and he and Patti left before the evening ended (and before he could honor a request to sing "Glory Days"!). But this humble and gracious act proved once again that Bruce is a regular, down-to-earth man at heart.

At the beginning of the new year, Bruce performed a show at the historic Count Basie Theater in Red Bank, New Jersey. Called Come Together, it was a benefit for slain police officer Patrick King. The show was arranged by fellow New Jersey rock idol Jon Bon Jovi and featured several Jersey artists, including Southside Johnny, Little Steven, Bobby Bandiera, Clarence Clemons, Max Weinberg, Patti Scialfa, and others.

"My Father's House"

On April 26, 1998, Bruce's father died. "There ain't a note I play on stage that can't be traced back directly to my mother and father," said Bruce in 1978. Judging from countless heartfelt songs on numerous albums, this cannot be denied. At the time of the elder Springsteen's death, Bruce said, "My father and I have had a very loving relationship. I feel lucky to have been so close to my dad as I became a man and father myself."

By late 1997, Bruce had made another record, sometimes referred to as "The Ghost of Tom Joad,

Part 2," because of its musical and lyrical similarity to 1995's *Tom Joad* album. But for reasons unknown—maybe Bruce was cautious about putting out yet another dark, acoustic album—the project was shelved. Instead, Bruce decided to embark on a project he'd been dreaming of for nearly twenty years—a collection of all the outtakes from his various albums since 1972. These were the tracks that didn't make a given album's final cut, and there were nearly 300 of them! This became the four-CD boxed set known as *Tracks,* released in November 1998.

"My Beautiful Reward"

When *Tracks* was finally released, it became the only box set to ever debut at number one on the *Billboard* charts. *Tracks* covers more than twenty-five years of Bruce's career and features a phenomenal sixty-six songs—fifty-six of which were previously unreleased. He planned to follow this up with a tour that reunited the original E Street Band. Boss fans, needless to say, were ecstatic.

On March 15, 1999, Bruce Springsteen was inducted into the Rock and Roll Hall of

Patti Scialfa, Clarence Clemons, and Steven Van Zandt flank Bruce during his induction into the Rock and Roll Hall of Fame in 1999.

Fame at a ceremony at the Waldorf Astoria Hotel in New York City. Bono of U2 gave the induction speech. However, the E Street Band was not included in this honor, which greatly upset fans, many of whom wrote letters to express their displeasure with the Rock and Roll Hall of Fame for excluding the band from

Did You Know?

In late February 1999, Bruce performed "Working on the Highway" on *Late Night with Conan O'Brien* before taking the house band's drummer, E Streeter Max Weinberg, back with him to New Jersey for tour rehearsals.

Bruce's induction. However, Bruce invited the entire E Street Band onstage to share in accepting the award; later that evening, they performed four songs for the crowd at the ceremony. This was the full band's first performance for an audience since September 1995. A few days later, Bruce and the E Street Band performed two rehearsal shows at the Convention Hall in Asbury Park. Bruce called the shows "the rebirth of the E Street Band."

The long-awaited 1999–2000 Springsteen World Tour finally began on April 9 in Barcelona, Spain.

For the next few months, the E Street Band traveled through Europe, playing thirty-six shows in twenty-six cities. A stand of fifteen sold-out homecoming shows at the Meadowlands in New Jersey began on July 15, 1999. The tour continued from New Jersey to cities all over the East Coast through the fall. Bruce made sure to play many songs that had not been heard live in decades.

On September 23, 1999, while touring, Bruce turned fifty years old. The 1999 leg of the Springsteen World Tour ended in Minneapolis, Minnesota, but Bruce told the crowd there to expect him and the band back on the road in 2000.

"Land of Hope and Dreams"

During the globe-trotting reunion tour, Bruce and the E Street Band thrilled fans with passionate shows, almost all of which lasted three hours or longer. Better still, Bruce said that the E Street Band was reunited for good. "I think the central thing for me right now is I'd really like to make a record with the band," Bruce said. "It's a

Bruce rocks out at Madison Square Garden on June 12, 2000.

Cover Me

Hundreds of artists have covered Bruce Springsteen's songs. Here are just a few of the numerous songs that have been covered by other bands and performers.

"Across the Border"	Emmylou Harris and Linda Ronstadt
"All I Need"	Gary U.S. Bonds
"All or Nothing at All"	Marshall Crenshaw
"All the Way Home"	Southside Johnny and the Asbury Jukes
"Atlantic City"	Hank Williams III
"Because the Night"	Patti Smith Group
"Because the Night"	The Waterboys
"The Big Payback"	Mojo Nixon
"Born to Run"	Frankie Goes to Hollywood
"Brilliant Disguise"	Elvis Costello
"Downbound Train"	The Smithereens

"The E Street Shuffle"	Bette Midler
"The Ghost of Tom Joad"	Rage Against the Machine
"Growin' Up"	David Bowie
"I'm On Fire"	Tori Amos
"Johnny 99"	Los Lobos
"Mansion on the Hill"	Billy Bragg
"My Father's House"	Cowboy Junkies
"My Father's House"	Ben Harper
"Pink Cadillac"	Natalie Cole
"Protection"	Donna Summer
"Racing in the Street"	Emmylou Harris
"Sad Eyes"	Enrique Iglesias
"State Trooper"	Cowboy Junkies
"Streets of Philadelphia"	Richie Havens
"Tougher than the Rest"	Everything But the Girl
"Tougher than the Rest"	Cher
"Used Cars"	Ani DiFranco
"Wreck on the Highway"	John Wesley Harding

different thought process when I think about writing for that group of musicians. I expand my scope, maybe, in some fashion. It's something about what the band is, after all these years, that makes me think a little bit different. I'm excited about doing that again."

One of Bruce's new songs was the controversial "American Skin (41 Shots)," written as a tribute to Guinean-American Amadou Diallo, who was killed in a hail of bullets by New York City police in February 1999. While fans appreciated Bruce's ongoing commitment to social issues, others protested the song. In fact, several police organizations called for a boycott of Bruce's music and concerts. "I was just setting out to basically continue writing about things that I'd written about for a long period of time, which is 'Who are we? What's it mean to be an American? What's going on in the country we live in?'" Bruce said at the time.

The final World Tour performances were captured on the newest album, *Live in New York City*. It debuted in April 2001 at number five on the *Billboard* album chart. A concert special was filmed exclusively for HBO, and a video/DVD version of the HBO show was also planned.

"Follow That Dream"

Bruce performed on Sunday, May 27, 2001, before 2,500 fans at the Stone Pony in Asbury Park. The show marked the one-year anniversary of the reopening of the revamped rock landmark. In the nearby town of Manalapan, a tornado was brewing. But onstage at the Pony, a whole other kind of tempest was taking place: "Every time he hits the stage, there's a storm," said Stone Pony owner Domenic Santana. "That's not Mother Nature. He just creates his own."

SELECTED DISCOGRAPHY

1973 *Greetings From Asbury Park, N.J.*

1973 *The Wild, The Innocent & the E Street Shuffle*

1975 *Born to Run*

1978 *Darkness on the Edge of Town*

1980 *The River*

1982 *Nebraska*

1984 *Born in the U.S.A.*

1986 *Bruce Springsteen & the E Street Band Live/1975–85*

1987 *Tunnel of Love*

1992 *Human Touch*

1992 *Lucky Town*

1995 *Greatest Hits*

1995 *The Ghost of Tom Joad*

1998 *Tracks*

2001 *Bruce Springsteen & the E Street Band: Live in New York City*

GLOSSARY

acclaim Praise or applause.

acoustic Without electricity; music played without instruments being "plugged in."

crooner A person who sings softly.

demo A recording intended to showcase a song or performer to a record producer.

disenfranchised Those deprived of a legal right or of some privilege or immunity, oftentimes the right to vote.

duet A song with two performers.

eclectic Having elements of different sources.

exhaustion An extreme feeling of being tired.

exuberant Extremely enthusiastic or joyful.

fraud Intentional twisting of the truth in order to induce another to part with something of value or to surrender a legal right.

icon Something that is worshiped; an object of devotion.

industrial Relating to labor or skill put toward the creation of something of value.

interspersed Mixed among other things.

obscure Not easily seen or understood.

phenomenal Exceptionally or unusually remarkable.

populist A believer in the rights, wisdom, or virtues of the common people.

sessions Periods of time spent within a recording studio to record musical tracks.

tempest A violent storm.

TO FIND OUT MORE

Backstreets
P.O. Box 11079
Washington, DC 20008
(800) 326-BOSS (2677)
Web site: http://www.backstreets.com

Rock and Roll Hall of Fame and Museum
One Key Plaza
Cleveland, OH 44114
(888) 764-ROCK (7625)
Web site: http://www.rockhall.com

Web Sites

The Boots Springsteen Home Page
http://home.theboots.net/theboots/home.html

Greasy Lake: The Ultimate Bruce Springsteen
Tribute Page
http://www.greasylake.org/greasy.htm

FOR FURTHER READING

Alterman, Eric. *It Ain't No Sin to Be Glad You're Alive: The Promise of Bruce Springsteen.* New York: Little, Brown & Company, 1999.

Cullen, Jim. *Born in the USA: Bruce Springsteen and the American Tradition.* New York: HarperCollins Publishers, 1998.

Editors of *Rolling Stone. Bruce Springsteen: The Rolling Stone Files.* New York: Hyperion, 1996.

Eliot, Marc, and Mike Appel. *Down Thunder Road: The Making of Bruce Springsteen.* New York: Simon and Schuster, 1992.

Goddard, Peter. *Bruce Springsteen Here and Now.* Hauppauge, NY: Barron's Educational Series, 1988.

Horn, Jeff. *Hungry Heart: The Music of Bruce Springsteen.* Bloomington, IN: 1st Books Library, 2000.

Marsh, Dave. *Born to Run: The Bruce Springsteen Story, Vol. 1.* New York: Thunder's Mouth Press, 1996.

Springsteen, Bruce. *Bruce Springsteen: Songs*. New York: Avon, 1998.

Works Cited

Bria, Amy. "Bruce Springsteen Takes the Stone Pony by Storm." *Asbury Park Press*, May 28, 2001.

Cocks, Jay. "Rock's New Sensation: The Backstreets Phantom of Rock." *Time*, October 27, 1975.

Duffy, John W. *Bruce Springsteen: In His Own Words*. New York: Omnibus Press, 2000.

Graff, Gary. "E for Effort: Bruce Springsteen Says the E Street Band Is Back to Stay." Reuters, 2001.

Landau, Jon. "Growing Young with Rock and Roll." *The Real Paper*, May 22, 1974.

Orth, Maureen, Janet Huck, and Peter S. Greenberg. "Making of a Rock Star." *Newsweek*, October 27, 1975.

Sandford, Christopher. *Springsteen Point Blank*. New York: Da Capo Press, 1999.

Wieder, Judy. "Bruce Springsteen: The Advocate Interview." *The Advocate*, May 1996.

INDEX

Bruce Springsteen

About the Author

Susie Derkins grew up in Monmouth County, New Jersey, and attended schools in the Freehold Regional High School District. A vinyl collector and folk artist, Susie lives in New York City's East Village. She thinks the Stone Pony is cool, but her favorite thing in Asbury Park is the Salvation Army.

Photo Credits

Cover, p. 5 © Bettman/Corbis; pp. 4, 9, 30–31, 32 © Corbis; pp. 7, 18, 26, 45, 64, 80 © Michael Ochs Archive; p. 10 © Hulton/Archive by Getty Images; pp. 14–15 © Jeff Albertson/Corbis; pp. 20, 76–77 © Henry Diltz/Corbis; pp. 22, 39, 43, 60, 71, 82, 88, 90, 92, 93, 96, 99 © AP/Wide World Photos; pp. 28, 41, 51 by Cindy Reiman; pp. 56, 67 © Everett Collection; p. 58 © Jacques M. Chenet/Corbis; p. 73 © John Cavanaugh.

Design

Thomas Forget

Layout

Tahara Hasan